Marketplace Jesus

Called and Anointed to Do Business!
An Abbreviated Biblical Survey

Bishop Ralph L. Dennis, Jr.

Copyright © 2003, 2005 by Ralph L. Dennis

Requests for information should be addressed to:
Ralph L. Dennis Ministries
6419 York Road
Baltimore, MD 21212

Marketplace Jesus
by Ralph L. Dennis

Printed in the United States of America

ISBN 1-59781-425-3

All rights reserved solely by the author. The author guarantees all contents are original and do not infringe upon the legal rights of any other person or work. No part of this book may be reproduced in any form without the permission of the author. The views expressed in this book are not necessarily those of the publisher.

Unless otherwise indicated, Bible quotations are taken from King James Version. Copyright ©1994 by World Bible Publishers.

www.xulonpress.com

Table of Contents

Preface vii

Introduction xiii

Chapter 1
    The Early Church and the Market place 15

Chapter 2
    Hidden in the Pews 17

Chapter 3
    All are Ministers Called to Preach? 19

Chapter 4
    We're All Kings and Priests 23

Chapter 5
    Getting into the Game 27

Chapter 6
   What is the Anointing? 29

Chapter 7
   A New Paradigm 33

Chapter 8
   The Disciple and the Marketplace 41

Chapter 9
   The God of Ministry is also the God of Business 51

Chapter 10
   Context and Capacity 59

Discovering and Living Your Purpose 69

Plan of Assurance for Those in the Marketplace 77

Preface

From the time that I was five years old, I knew with some level of certainty that I would be a preacher. It was then that I recall having, what I know now to be an open vision. I saw Christ and me standing on the highway. I was praying, pleading, and pointing people to Him. Being raised in a family that was quite spiritual that was not too devastating until I started becoming of age and understanding that I had other choices.

In my familiar environment, preachers were some of the most learned; although their educations were not a gateway to anything but the science and art of preaching and teaching the Word of God. Every preacher I knew was either a person who preached and worked other jobs or one who was far below the poverty line (poor). Yet, they were to be considered a witness. Apparently, it was a demonstration of one's witness and satisfaction in being a servant of the Lord, knowing that "the Lord will make a way, somehow!"

I realized by the time I reached high school and had to begin to consider a career, that I did not like the "poor thing." So even though I had given the Lord my heart and loved Him with all that I knew,

Marketplace Jesus

preaching would have to be a secondary career. I had been working since I was five years old and liked the idea of having money and preachers where I lived did not have much. Not only that, but also by high school, I was aware that what I had learned in church made me a real talent in school. In church, I had learned to sing, speak before groups, lead a small group of my peers, and interface with those older than myself. I was exposed to many things in church and therefore was more comfortable doing certain things in school than many of my peers.

I was blessed to finish high school as the class salutatorian and got a scholarship to go to college. This was a real challenge since I did not know many people who attended college other than my teachers. At that time, I had one cousin who was in college. The only other person close to me who had a college degree was a teacher (by day) and preacher (by night) who directed the youth choir at church. But, I saw no future in my community, so college was the way out.

In college, the scale was raised to a level I had never known. I was considered smart and quite gifted back home, but at college everybody was. For the first time, I felt intimidated. My clothes were inferior. The academic curriculum I had completed was inferior. My family's background was grossly different. My perspective about the choices of what I could be and do was quite narrow compared to what others were seeking to become.

For the first time, preaching for a living got pushed further and further out of my mind. Not only was it not popular, but it was the poorest career path being pursued among any of my new peers. So, I decided to pursue a degree in mathematics. It was a compromise, but I lacked the sciences for a medical career. My claim to success was driven by the published claim that math graduates have more diversity in their career choices than any other graduates because of their ability to think logically.

After marriage, one child, and graduation from college, I continued a career in banking for a short time. I then got the break I had been looking for a chance to go into sales and marketing. In corporate America, I worked diligently for major companies, making my mark as I strived for "success." I did not forget God or my work of ministry; however, life as a full time preacher became less and less a desire as I began to earn more and more money and acquire more and more things. To satisfy both my will and the will of the Lord, I accepted a pastorate while working as a regional sales manager and continued to climb both the corporate ladder and the ladder of leadership in my denomination. WOW! This was the best of both worlds until that "still small voice" I had heard at five years old began to speak very loudly again.

For a number of years, I was able to ignore the Lord's voice as it pertained to fulltime ministry. My ignoring God became disobedience, and near rebellion. I was so determined to stay in corporate America that the Lord started orchestrating troubles in my career and I knew it. Soon, I had no choice but to step out on faith in His word and submit to a calling that was before me since I was five. I have often said to others my problem was not in trusting the Lord, it was in trusting the Lord's people. I knew the little church I was pastoring could not pay me what I was making, so I decided to "help God" by creating a couple of business ventures. Well, to my chagrin, on May 31, 1991, the building that housed my businesses caught fire, destroying most of what I had. This was the hand of God and I knew it, so I yielded.

It has taken years to get back to the salary level I had in corporate America, but not back to the flow of blessing. Little became much as I yielded my life more and more each day to the purpose for which He had made me. Favor became a manifestation of His provision in every area of my life. Now, I can share with many others the process and the necessity of choosing and obeying the call of God on their lives.

What I did not understand then was why I was even allowed to stay in Corporate America long as I did. As I look retrospectively, I was there for a season and for a reason. I was there as the "church" in the Kingdom, though at that time my knowledge of that was limited. I was there as a light in darkness; as an evangelist of the gospel; as the salt of the earth. All of those are great reasons! The only problem was that it was not the ultimate place where God wanted me. It was part of the process to be an apostle in the body of Christ.

Now that I am aware of the Kingdom being the domain of the King, I can use all that I learned in the kingdoms of this world to assist others in how to maximize their time as the good seed in the field, the world. I understand that others, like myself, will not remain there forever, but I am also very confident that most who understand ministry will find their daily place of vocation to be their sphere of rule and influence.

My quest is to teach them how to optimize their presence as apostles, prophets, evangelists, pastors, and teachers in the marketplace. Conjunctively, it is my role to change the measure of value that the local church has set in determining the contribution, and ultimately the worth we assign to those in the pulpits versus those in the market. This means that we must reassess spiritual callings and what venues we are anointed to effect.

We are called to be the Church in the Kingdom. We must be aware of this, and make this our ministry 24 hours a day, 7 days a week, without exception. It is not to be the work of few, but all who believe that Jesus Christ is both Savior and Lord. As this happens in the marketplaces throughout the world, then will we hear and witness that "the kingdoms of this world are become the kingdoms of our Lord and of His Christ, and He shall reign forever and forever. Amen."

Introduction

One of my favorite scriptures that relates to the marketplace is Matthew 13: 36-43, where the disciples follow Jesus home to get clarity on the parable that they heard Him teach regarding the tares of the field. Jesus points out to them several truths I find quite significant for the work of ministry in the 21st century church. Look at what He says:

1. He that sows the good seed is the Son of man.
2. The field is the world.
3. The good seed are the children of the kingdom.
4. The tares are the children of the wicked one.
5. The enemy that sowed them (tares) is the devil.
6. The harvest is the end of the world.
7. The reapers are the angels.

From this parable, explained again in Luke 8: 9-15, we see that ***"the good seed is the word of God."*** As we compare the texts of Matthew and Luke, I believe we can safely conclude that the children of the kingdom (the good seed) are to be sown into the field (the world), as the Word of God.

In today's terms, we are simply saying that God wants the Church in the Kingdom, the marketplace. To appreciate this, we must accurately define both the Church and the Kingdom, as to not exclude from the kingdom anything created.

For the sake of simplicity, I consider the marketplace any setting outside the usual nomenclature of the local church that presents to the saints an opportunity to minister. This includes businesses of all magnitudes, every level of education, and governmental departments and agencies. In the synergy center design that I have for the community, I call them sheep gates or connectives that get the Truth in every social, medical, economical, educational, and political setting (S.H.E.E.P.), based on faith.

This must become the posture of The New Ethnic, the community of Believers in the Lord Jesus Christ. Every believer must understand his calling as a minister, and develop a confidence in his ability to minister with wisdom in whatever place in the market God calls him to. The power and authority of the Church must shift from the pulpit to the pews; from the few to the many; from some to all. For us not to do this leaves all creation at risk.

CHAPTER 1

The Early Church in the Marketplace

The marketplace was the center of activity for the Early Church and its ministry. There seemed to be for them no struggle with this since they gathered there regularly to conduct business. Once they found relationship with Jesus and began following Him, they then witnessed to unbelievers in the marketplace. This was the place where they performed signs and wonders. Unlike the Church today, all except one of the twenty-two power encounters in the book of Acts took place outside of a conventional religious setting. The one found in Acts 3 took place inside the Temple, but immediately impacted the marketplace because the men who carried the lame man daily from his home to the gate and back were suddenly unemployed.

Throughout the Acts spiritual demonstrations of power were facilitated by business people like Priscilla and Aquila, Lydia and, most of all, a scholar and businessman named Saul who had a name change. Their professions became the place of their witness. They did not have a Bible, tracts to hand out or mass media to distribute their testimonies. They used the workplace to tell others what they had seen, heard, and experienced. Thus, the marketplace was the primary rock-bed in the founding and growth of the first century New Testament Church.

It is also quite remarkable that the early followers of Christ did not give up their businesses. It seems that they remained in business, while at the same time, involving themselves in the full-time work of ministry. This was due, I believe, to the fact that the marketplace was their parish and their businesses were their pulpit. Sharing the love of Jesus, telling others what they experienced, and word of mouth witnessing were not special efforts, but a lifestyle.

CHAPTER 2

Hidden in the Pews

When we gather in churches across the country on any given Sunday, there are millions more in the pews then there are in the pulpits. Yet, it seems to me that the hope of the masses to accomplish the Great Commission is placed on the elite few who have access to a microphone. If there is any recognition, it is directed to those who exercise their work of ministry primarily within the walls of the local church, while literally millions of men, women, boys and girls called to minister, go unrecognized because their destiny is in the marketplace. This must change quickly.

Though most probably would not announce it, these masses often feel second best or not very important compared to those who serve in a church context. Over the years, no one has addressed their contributions outside the walls of the church unless it was something generally accepted as church, such as outreach, missions, retreats, and etc. Consequently, we have no way to measure or qualify any contribution they make as the Church in the Kingdom. They go from CEOs and Executive managers on Monday through Friday to an unknown, dispensable, perpetually spiritual adolescent on Sunday. This is not only unfair, but it arms the enemy. We now allow the kingdom of darkness to claim what is the Lord's. We reinforce it when we allow the only praise that these generals of the marketplace get is in the marketplace. In this season, we must not only cause them to realize that it is okay to do ministry in the marketplace, but that God has deliberately called them and anointed them for it.

They have been chosen and empowered by the Holy Spirit for a divinely sanctioned assignment in what we normally refer to as a secular setting. Many of these individuals perceive that there is a connection between their business and ministry, but do not know exactly how. Even though they sense a call to ministry, they hesitate about exchanging their secular setting for a religious one. Quite often they are told that this vacillation is due to a lack of faith, or worse yet, attachment to worldly things. This indictment leaves them confused because they sense that their spiritual destiny is in the marketplace. If, they ultimately leave the church, we console our religious posture by misquoting scriptures like "it's as hard for a rich man to get into heaven as it is for a camel to go through the eye of a needle."

CHAPTER 3

Are All Ministers Called to Preach?

I believe one of the most over looked text in the Bible might be Mark 16: 15-18. This word was not left to a few charismatic leaders in the church, but to everybody in the pews as well. Let us look at what Jesus said. *"Go ye into all the world, and preach the gospel to every creature. He that believeth and is baptized shall be saved; but he that believeth not shall be damned. And these signs shall follow them that believe; in my name shall they cast out devils; they shall speak with new tongues; They shall take up serpents; and if they drink any deadly thing, it shall not hurt them; they shall lay hands on the sick, and they shall recover."*

This sets the pattern for the New Testament Church. Consequently, in the first century we discover that percentage-wise, more people did ministry in the marketplace than in religious settings. They did more than witness, they brought transformation to the villages and cities they lived in or visited.

Today, marketplace ministers fail to rise to their God-appointed positions because they are often derided as "untrained and uneducated" by the standards of the religious system. The same thing happened to Peter and John. They were businessmen/ministers who were referred to as unlearned by those who heard them in the religious settings. The deciding factor to become a minister is not religious education, but spiritual conditioning that comes from "having been with Jesus" (Acts 4:13).

The first century Apostles were ministering businessmen who had been spiritually conditioned, and according to Acts 5:28, they were able to fill Jerusalem with their doctrine in just a few weeks. As a result, Jerusalem experienced transformation at the deepest levels; the needs of the poor and the widows were met. These were two vulnerable groups. The hungry were fed and the sick were healed. Even the Sanhedrin, the most powerful forum among the Jews, was positively influenced by the Gospel. Solomon's Portico became the place for a steady stream of signs and wonders, giving the emerging church favor with the people (note Acts 5:12-15).

They Took It To The Streets

The movement was so dynamic that eventually the streets and sidewalks of Jerusalem were turned into evangelistic venues as sick people were lined up hoping for the healing shadow of Peter to fall on them (Acts 5:15-16). Soon afterwards multitudes from nearby cities literally flooded Jerusalem. What a change! This city that had grieved Jesus to the point of tears was now giving Him joy.

It all began when the disciples left the confines of the Upper Room for the open space of the marketplace on the Day of Pentecost. Peter, the fisherman, became the first fisher of men, setting a pattern soon to be duplicated all over the Roman Empire.

The key is this: (as recorded by a doctor) this movement was not led by men notorious for their religious acumen, but by people known for their place in the marketplace as fishermen, tax collectors, and farmers.

Business Partners Transform the City

Before long a myriad of towns and cities were touched, culminating in Ephesus, a site of the most dramatic power encounter in the book of Acts (note Acts 19: 1-13). This city, with a demon driven economy and a marketplace that was the citadel of evil, experienced the most radical transformation. At the center of the transformation were Paul, Aquila, and Priscilla, who in addition to preaching the word of God, were partners in business. This dual status connected them to the religious community through their teaching and to the marketplace by their tent-making enterprise. The positioning of these three anointed business people could not have been more strategic. It is no wonder the marketplace in Ephesus was so powerfully affected.

Street Recruiting

From the beginning, the marketplace has been friendly territory as far as God is concerned. Jesus, a recognized businessman (Mark 6: 3), recruited His disciples there, not in the temple. None of the Twelve was a member of the professional clergy or a leader in the synagogue. It is true that later on many of the priests joined the Church and Paul's addition brought on board one of the best rabbis of the day (Acts 6:7; 9:1-16), but he was also a businessman, who as the need arose, ran a profitable business. In Ephesus, his business was large enough to provide for him, his team and needy people as well (Acts 20:33-35).

The elders of the emerging churches were usually marketplace leaders. Often they were the result of dramatic conversions, as in the case of Dorcas, Lydia and Cornelius that produced conversion movements, most likely due to their prominence in the city (Acts 9:36-43; 10:1-48; 16:14-21).

CHAPTER 4

We're All Kings and Priests

According to Revelations 1:6, we have all been made to be kings and priests unto God. Although it has not been generally accepted by the church, I am convinced that this is our position in Christ. Not just for a few either, but for every believer.

Most religious leaders today have very little interaction with unbelievers, even less so with prominent ones. The church does not command the attention or the respect of the marketplace. In fact, quite often it is considered irrelevant and seen as some sort of social parasite. To compound this misconception, the church members who do have relevance in the city on account of their position in the marketplace tend to disqualify themselves from leadership in spiritual matters. The most common self-inflicted putdown is "I am not a pastor; I am just a layman." All of this is a clever satanic scheme to neutralize the apostles, prophets, evangelists, pastors, and teachers, along with an entire army of disciples, already positioned in the marketplace.

Some people are called to serve inside the church, and this is a precious call. They are the modern equivalent of the Old Testament priests who ministered in the Temple, but others are anointed to serve in the city, like the kings of the same period. There are some who have an anointing to do both. Whether you are called to both or one is not an issue, for both calls are valid and interdependent. Unfortunately, the former has been exalted to the detriment of the latter. Whether people are priests in the temple or kings in society, they all partake of the same calling as ministers of God.

Spiritual Warfare in the Boardroom

Businesspeople also need to know that spiritual warfare is a central component of the daily routine, whether they are aware of it or not. Satan and his evil forces are constantly trying to destroy lives and enterprises in the church, but even more so in the city. The extraordinary opposition Christian businesspeople experience when putting deals together in a godly way is no different than what pastors face when counseling suicidal people or those contemplating divorce. The solution is one and the same: believers willing to minister in the power of the Holy Spirit to those oppressed by the devil in order to set them free and to turn the spiritual tide. The location is ancillary.

When believers in the marketplace are reduced to second-class status, the church is automatically deprived of its most strategically placed soldiers because they are the ones closest to satan's command and control centers. If properly equipped, they can do lethal damage to the systems by which the devil holds people captive in our cities. This is why he allocates so much of his resources to make them feel unqualified and inferior in spiritual matters.

Four Lethal Misbelieves

It is the combination of four main misbelieves that allows the devil to neutralize God's calling on those anointed for business:

- that there is a God ordained division between clergy and laity.

- that the church is called to operate primarily inside a building often referred to as the temple.

- that people involved in business cannot be as spiritual as those serving in church ministry are.

- that the primary role of businesspeople is to make money to support the vision of the ministry."

There are multitudes of people out there who need to know that they are a vital part of God's Kingdom on earth because without their active participation and leadership, our cities will not be transformed and the Great Commission will not be fulfilled in our generation.

CHAPTER 5

Getting in the Game

Too often ministry in the church resembles what goes on during the final match in the Playoffs: a handful of players on the field who are in desperate need of rest, while hundreds of thousands of spectators, who can use the exercise, watch from comfortable seats. The players are the "ministers" who have the "right" to be on the playing field. The spectators are the "lay people" whose participation is limited to a secondary role, mainly making the whole enterprise financially feasible.

This unbiblical classification of church membership results in first and second class status in God's Kingdom. This should not be so because Jesus was not an elitist. Even though He recruited 12 apostles and appointed them to positions of leadership, He was always inclusive. When He spoke, except when He addressed specific situations pertaining to the Twelve, He invariably spoke to and for everybody.

This division has to be eliminated if we are to fulfill the Great Commission. No one is more strategically positioned in the city than Christians operating in the marketplace. God has already given them jurisdiction in businesses, schools, and government circles. The promise that "Every place on which the sole of your foot treads, I have given it to you" (Jos. 1:3) applies to them also-and they tread all over the city on a daily basis!

If, You are in Position, Go for it!

Christians who have been anointed for business are strategically positioned already. The Lord is in their hearts. The Holy Spirit is imbuing their spirits. The word is planted in their minds. All they need now is to realize that they are anointed to operate in the fullness of God in the business world and begin to walk in that anointing. Then, they will be able to push back the satanic infrastructure controlling our cities and take important steps to establishing the Kingdom of God on earth. When this happens, the whole world will hear the voice of God.

CHAPTER 6

What is the Anointing?

To be anointed for business is to be set aside by God to minister in the marketplace in the fullness of the Holy Spirit in order to take the gospel to every creature by using our jobs as the main ministry vehicle (Mark 16:15).

Anointing is an important subject in the Scriptures that is often associated with oil. Pouring, rubbing, or smearing something or someone with oil was the way to indicate that a person, an item, or a place had been set aside, for divine use. In the Bible when a person was anointed, a large amount of oil- symbol of the Holy Spirit – was poured on the head to symbolize that the totality of the person was set aside. In the Scriptures, the anointing was always for full-time consecration. Kings, priests, prophets, and places were set aside, in total for divine service. Part-time anointing, or anointing for part-time ministry, is not found in the Bible.

In the Bible, the anointing is always abundant, never scarce. In Psalm 133:1-3, we are shown the picture of oil running down the head, the beard, and eventually the robe of Aaron. The passage compares the anointing to the dew of Hermon, which comes down upon the mountains of Zion. Abundant, overflowing, enveloping, transforming anointing is what we see in this Psalm. This is precisely what God has in mind for people in the marketplace. To anoint them with so much of Him that they will "open (their) eyes so they (sinners) will turn from darkness to light and from the dominion of satan to God" (Acts 26:18a). This anointing is meant to transform people and their environment as implied by the next statement: "In order that they may receive forgiveness of sins and an inheritance among those who have been sanctified by faith in God" (Acts 26:18b).

Gifts in the Marketplace

Furthermore, Jesus' promise that believers will be filled with the Holy Spirit, cast out demons, expose lurking threats (serpents), survive evil schemes (surreptitious poisonous drinks), and make sick things well, (Mark 16:17,18) has to do primarily with service in the marketplace. This is so, for at least two reasons: First, the context for Jesus' words is the command to "Go ye into all the world and preach the gospel to every creature" (Mk. 16:15). The process described by Jesus is definitely centrifugal and expansive. The entire world, the totality of creation, is the focus of our mission, not just a church building, or a gathering of believers.

Second, only demons with suicidal tendencies would dare hang around Spirit-filled church meetings. Most demons spend the bulk of their time in the pernicious command centers that control our cities- the still unredeemed business, educational, and governmental circles. It is precisely in those places where God's power is desperately needed. And who is already strategically positioned to channel it? Those called to minister in the marketplace.

Marketplace Jesus

These men and women have always had the desire to do something extraordinary for God, but they have been stopped by the limitations and the resulting shame – imposed on them by the old paradigms.

In the past, they had seen themselves as spiritual "Prisoners Of War", desperately trying to survive with dignity in an evil environment. Because they were taught that the marketplace was off limits to the kingdom of God, the best they dared hope for was to be good witnesses and maybe lead someone to Christ. They never felt empowered to embrace the possibility of seeing the marketplace transformed. Consequently, the notion of the kingdom of God materializing in their midst to displace the evil kingdom, lay beyond the outer limits of their expectations. Consequently, they settled for merely living an honorable life in a dishonorable environment.

CHAPTER 7

A New Paradigm

However, when the pivotal role of the marketplace in God's plan is unveiled, a new paradigm emerges. Businesspeople soon discover that in the same fashion that pastors are able to minister God's transforming power to individuals and to domestic institutions (marriages and families), they can also minister to the people and the secular institutions that operate in the marketplace. All of a sudden, the marketplace ceases to be a stronghold of the devil to be avoided; it becomes a ministry to stage its spiritual transformation. To better understand this, we need to see how Jesus viewed the marketplace and His role in it.

Jesus and the Marketplace

What was Jesus' relationship with the marketplace? We tend to see Him as antagonistic to it because of what He did to the temple merchants or by reason of His suggestion to the wealthy young ruler to give away his possessions. Was He really hostile towards business and wealth? What was His attitude really like?

Marketplace Jesus

Traditionally, we picture Him as remote and removed, more as a monk than as a manager. However, because of the roles He embodied – ruler, teacher, and businessman - Jesus belongs in the marketplace rather than in a monastery.

We easily see Him as a teacher by virtue of how well He taught and because in the Gospels He is referred to as a Rabbi. We also recognize Him as the ultimate ruler because He is the King of kings. However, picturing Him as a businessman is where we have the most difficulty. Yet, in the gospels the opposite was true. At first, Jesus was more easily recognized as a businessman than as a rabbi or a ruler.

Jesus was Born in the Marketplace

Jesus was in touch with the marketplace from the very beginning of His life on Earth for He was born in a place of business, an inn (Luke 2:7). The angelic worship service to celebrate His birth, took place in a nearby feeding lot (Luke 2: 13- 14).

Rather than religious leaders, Jesus' first visitors consisted of employees and small business owners including shepherds (Luke 2:15-20), which His parents received in the inn's parking lot. I say this because the manger was the equivalent of the modern gas stations since it was used to dispense "fuel" (food) to the mules and donkeys (vehicles), and to provide a place of rest (parked) for the night.

All of these events could have happened in the temple or in its courts. Instead, God, in His sovereignty chose secular venues for them. I believe this was intended to show God's heart for the marketplace, where sinners, the object of His love, spend the bulk of their time. Another reason could be that God wanted Jesus to get in touch with the heart of the city, the marketplace, from the very beginning of His earthly life. Later on He identified even more by becoming a businessman.

Jesus, The Businessman

Shortly after He began to preach, His neighbors in Nazareth asked, "Is not this the carpenter, the son of Mary, and brother of James and Joses, and Juda, and Simon? Are not His sisters here with us? And they were offended at Him" (Mark 6:3). Please notice how they described Him by his occupation, "the carpenter" but refused to see Him as a credible teacher and much less as a ruler. Such possibilities caused them to take offense at Him perhaps because they could not accept a local businessman as credible in spiritual matters.

It was not difficult for those neighbors to see Jesus as a businessman since many may have engaged in His professional services. A carpenter, in biblical times, was a builder who used primarily wood. I suspect that many of those folks ate at tables made by Jesus and secured their homes with doors built in His shop. Some of their houses could have had beams cut and fit by the Savior. Even some of their oxen may have worn Jesus-made harnesses. He did not do carpentry work occasionally, or in His spare time because like every boy in Israel, He was taught a trade in His teens, or even earlier. This means that by the time of His baptism He had been working at it for at least 20 years. He was no mere apprentice, but a well-established artisan.

Jesus, The Profitable Entrepreneur

Jesus did not do carpentry as a hobby either. He had been taught a trade in order to make a living and this required that He run His shop at a profit. Cost of goods, amount of labor required, the interplay between supply and demand, competitive pricing, return on investment, and replacement of equipment were all part of His business routine. Even though it may be hard for us to picture Jesus working for a profit, this is precisely what He did for most of His earthly life.

Nor did He do small-time carpentry just when He was short on money. Earlier on, most likely when Joseph his father was still alive, He was described as "the carpenter's son" (see Mt. 13:55). Now, His neighbors' description as "the" carpenter, and listing Him as the head of the family, seems to indicate that Joseph had passed away. If so, He was running a family owned business where as the firstborn He was the senior partner, His brothers were junior associates and His mother and sisters played supportive roles. This was not a small shop, but one large enough to provide a living for a family of eight or more of which Jesus was the leader (see Mk. 6:3).

Labor was a central part of Jesus' life because, according to Jewish tradition, as a Rabbi, He had to master a trade and exercise it honestly to support himself to be able to teach for free. His instruction to others that "it is more blessed to give than to receive," as quoted by Paul (see Acts 20:35), required that He had the means to acquire goods to be given away since He practiced what He preached.

Jesus, The Well-Informed Leader

The picture of an ascetic, hermit-like Jesus does not emerge from the Scriptures, but from distorted human traditions. It is true that He spent long hours alone in prayer, but He usually did this at night. During the day, He interacted with all sorts of people and His conversation incorporated the most diverse combination of business topics. He was definitely a very well-informed person and one who acquired information through direct exposure to things and situations.

Jesus, The Marketplace Connoisseur

His parables show that He was thoroughly familiar with the marketplace and its operation. His examples dealt with construction (Matt. 7:24-27); wine making (Luke 5: 37,38); farming (Mark 4: 2-20); treasure hunting (Matt. 13:44); ranching (Matt. 18: 12-14); management and labor (Matt. 20: 1-16); family owned businesses (Matt. 21: 28-31); hostile takeovers (Luke 20: 9-19); return on investments (Matt. 25: 14-30); future markets (Luke 12: 16-21); crop yield (Mark 4: 26-32); management criteria (Luke 12:35-48); the need for research (Luke 14: 24-35); bankruptcy (Luke 15: 11-16); the advantage of leverage (Luke 16: 1-13); and venture capital in high risk situations (Luke 19: 11-27).

Jesus, the Performer of Business Miracles

Many of Jesus' miracles took the form of business wonders. He produced a tremendous return on a young boy's investment by turning his few fish and loaves into a complete meal for thousands (Matt. 14:13; 15:23). The transformation of water into wine belongs in the same category (John 2:1-10) and shows Jesus' sympathy for those in charge of catering. His instructions leading to two miraculous catches of fish are the modern equivalent of an insightful stockbroker's advice (Luke 5: 1-14; John 20:1). Peter and his crew must have sold those fish for a profit since they were commercial fisherman. Furthermore, when tax time came, Jesus gave a hot tip to Peter to acquire the cash required to pay the bill for both of them (Matt. 17: 24).

Jesus, The Friend of Poor and Rich Alike

Jesus interacted liberally with poor people, but He was no stranger to the upper end of society. While a toddler, the Magi visited Him. These men who presented Him with very expensive gifts were wealthy professionals specializing in astronomy, medicine, and natural science.

He was often the guest of honor at parties offered by wealthy people (Luke 11: 37; 14:7; 19:5). One of them, Joseph of Arimathea provided a deluxe burial place for Jesus, a tomb hewn out in the rock, instead of the less expensive ones dug in the ground (Mt. 27:57-60). This Joseph, along with Gamaliel and Nicodemus, was a member of the Sanhedrin. This influential institution was the modern equivalent of the Chamber of Commerce, the Elks Club, and the President's Roundtable, rolled into one.

Also a group of wealthy women is reported as funding Jesus' ministry. This is mentioned right after He and the Twelve became itinerant preachers (Luke 8: 1,3). This may have become necessary because itinerant preaching must have taken them away from their regular jobs. These women contributed to the support of Jesus and the Twelve. Evidently, these ladies had significant wealth. This illustrates a point often missed, that Jesus befriended the wealthy as well as the poor.

Jesus Was Well Provided For

The notion that Jesus was perpetually broke is not Scriptural either. His robe was seamless, which made it the First Century equivalent of an Armani suit. It is true that His parents gave the poor man's offering when they presented Him to the Lord (Luke 2: 22–24), and that His statement about not having a place to lay His head could mean that He did not own much personally (Luke 9: 58), but He always had adequate resources for His ministry and for the support of those traveling with Him. The fact that Judas, the team treasurer, was able to steal money undetected suggests that there were plenty of funds on hand to provide cover for his pilfering (John 13:19).

Jesus was not a hermit, but one who operated with great comfort in the marketplace and who was known to have done honest work for a living. This is also true of His disciples. The notion that Jesus and His followers extracted themselves from society cannot be sustained from the Scriptures. They led intense and normal lives and not once did they dichotomize labor and spiritual matters.

The Interplay Between Labor and Worship

This is very important because work, in the Bible, is never presented as non-spiritual. In fact, God introduced labor before worship (Gen. 1:28). Not because labor was, or is, superior to worship, but in the Garden, labor was worship. Furthermore, after sin contaminated the soil, God pointed to labor as the way to deal with it. He told Adam, "Cursed is the ground because of you" (Gen. 3: 17, NIV), causing it to no longer yield its fruit spontaneously. At that moment, physical labor, toiling, and the sweat of the brow, were introduced as the redemptive tool to extract the now reluctant fruit.

Jesus, a businessman for over twenty years, recruited marketplace people to bring the kingdom of God to sinners in cities all over. He did this at the onset of the Church Age to establish a pattern, and He has yet to change His approach. He is a friend of the marketplace and of what goes on in it. This is why it is important to see how His disciples related to the marketplace.

CHAPTER 8

The Disciples & The Marketplace

How did Jesus' disciples relate to the marketplace? Jesus left no doubt that His mission was to overpower and destroy the devil's empire by putting an end to its destructive manifestations in the lives of people (Luke 4: 18-21). To accomplish this, He set out to create something new— the church (Matt. 16: 18-19). Jesus described it not as an abstract notion, but as a tangible gathering of people.

From the very beginning, Jesus reached outside of the rarified religious circles in Jerusalem to recruit His core group of disciples. These men became the human foundation for the divine social vehicle designed to change the world. Jesus' ultimate objective was not to see revival happen in the temple, or in the myriad of synagogues dotting the Roman Empire and beyond, but to transform society, and not just Jewish society, but society all over the world.

The Church as the Counterculture

For this He launched a movement that was meant to be the counterculture rather than a subculture. Subcultures are satisfied with surviving under the dominant culture. On the other hand, the counterculture has as its irretrievable objective to debunk and replace the prevailing culture.

Neither Jesus nor his Apostles ever described the members of the Church as individuals isolated and removed from everyday life. There were no monks in the Early Church. In fact, New Testament teaching is intentionally focused on repairing broken relationships and transforming society's institutions – marriage, family, work, and government. This is so because Jesus' mission was never to save isolated individuals, but to change the world.

The new movement is aimed at changing the world by changing the people living in it, primarily in its cities. And to accomplish this, it had to affect the cities' most vital component: the marketplace, with its combination of business, education, and government, the societal systems that define and give life to a metropolis.

Jesus' Apostles Came From the Marketplace

This is why Jesus recruited people from the marketplace to be the backbone of His movement. Even though He was a Rabbi, none of The Twelve was a leader in the temple or in the synagogue. John and James were partners with their father in a food enterprise. Peter had his own fishing company. Matthew was a tax officer. Nathaniel, whom Jesus saw sitting under a tree, was probably a farmer. Bypassing the religious circles was intentional on Jesus' part.

Marketplace Leaders Wrote the Gospels

The writing of the gospels, Christianity's most foundational documents, was entrusted not to religious scholars, but to marketplace leaders: a medical doctor (Luke); a retired tax officer (Matthew); a partner in a food enterprise (John); and, an unemployed millionaire (Mark).

I say this of Mark because there is evidence to suggest that he came from a wealthy family. His mother, Mary, was the one in whose house many gathered to pray for Peter's release from prison (Acts 12: 12-17). She must have had a large home to accommodate such a large gathering. When Peter knocked at the gate, Rhoda, a maidservant came to open it. Poor people do not own servants and their homes do not have gates, but rather doors abutting the street. Rhoda, startled, ran inside without opening the gate. Peter kept on knocking, but the house must have had an entranceway long enough for him not to be heard by those inside.

Later on, Mark flowed in ministry between Paul, Barnabas, and Peter. Maybe it was his comfortable upbringing that caused him to desert Barnabas in Pamphylia and not go with them to work (Acts 13: 13; 15: 38). Nevertheless, this wealthy scion was entrusted with the extraordinary privilege of writing one of the Gospels.

The Church Was Conceived in a Private Home

The church was not conceived – in the physiological sense of the word – inside a religious setting, such as the temple or the synagogue, but in a private home. The Upper Room, the place where they gathered during the "gestation period" was the spiritual equivalent of the human womb.

What was The Upper Room like? We usually picture it as nothing more than a large shack. In musicals and programs, it is depicted as a tiny place, no bigger than a small hut. But it must have been a very large place if 120 men and women were staying in it (see Acts 1: 13, 15). "Staying" means that they took their meals and slept in it. It is safe to assume that The Upper Room was possibly the largest room in a colossal villa-type residence owned by one of the wealthiest men in Jerusalem. The choice of such a secular venue for the gestation of the church must not be overlooked.

Marketplace Leaders:
The Backbone of The Early Church

The human backbone of The Early Church consisted of marketplace leaders, including new converts like Lydia, a wealthy wholesaler of expensive fabric, who had homes both in Philippi and in Thyatira. Dorcas, a notable businesswoman, was a designer and manufacturer of inner garments. Apparently, she must have made a good living from it, because "she was abounding with deeds of kindness and charity which she continually did" (Acts 9:36 NAS). The words "abounding and continually" speak of a high level of giving for which corresponding wealth is required. She was prominent enough for her death to be brought to the attention of Peter via a request for him to come and for her subsequent resurrection to be noticed by an entire town; and, for many of its citizens to believe in the Lord (Acts 9: 36-42).

Aquila and Priscilla were also businesspeople. They had the same profession as Paul: tentmakers. To us, the word tent evokes images of Boy Scout size tents, but in the First Century, tents were far more elaborate than that. To be a tentmaker was the equivalent of being a modern day developer of hotels since this is what tents were used for: temporary lodging away from home. In addition, tent-makers did all kinds of work using leather. One of their main clients may have been the Roman Army, since Ephesus had an important garrison.

Government Officials Were Early Disciples

Government officials were a part of the early church: The Ethiopian Eunuch and Erastus. The Ethiopian Eunuch was in charge of all the treasure of Candace, Queen of Ethiopia (see Acts 8:27). It is most unfortunate that we refer to him by his horrible man-inflicted handicap, instead of as the Finance Minister of a prominent kingdom. This shows our bias against the marketplace, in general, and prominent people in particular. I am sure that upon arriving in Ethiopia, it was his governmental position that enabled him to present the gospel to others –mainly people of influence- and not his degrading physical scars. Erastus is described by Paul as the city treasurer, definitely a very important position (Rom. 16: 23).

The Marketplace Produces Excellent Church Leaders

Community and marketplace people were leaders of the newly established churches. Their effectiveness as elders was extraordinary when one considers that they were appointed after a brief time of training and usually in a context of severe persecution. One cannot help but wonder how Paul managed to be so accurate in his selection of elders for the emerging congregations. The answer lies with the fact that these folks were already leaders in the city who, after coming to Christ through a power encounter, went on to lead the Church. And by leading, I mean more than sitting on a board of trustees. They presided over it and carried on ministry on a daily basis.

God did not hesitate to entrust marketplace leaders with complex theological issues either. The most controversial theological truth of the First Century – that Gentiles can be saved without having to become Jews first – was first presented to three marketplace leaders: Peter (food industry), Simeon the Tanner (leather goods), and

Cornelius, (military). This was a new and radical teaching for which the Church had no paradigm. Nevertheless, God did not hesitate to entrust it to "laymen." The fact that they had not been trained theologically, like the Pharisees, was an advantage rather than a disadvantage given the unprecedented nature of the new truth.

World Mission Centers Established in Trading Cities

When the time came to establish a missionary center to stage the spreading of the Gospel to the ends of the earth, God moved the spiritual vortex of the Church to Antioch, a merchant city located at the convergence of important trading roads.

Seven Community Leaders Chosen as Apostolic Co-workers

One of the most common misconceptions is to view the seven men chosen in Acts 6, as the equivalent of modern day deacons. In many Bible translations, the subtitle for this chapter is "Election of Deacons." In fact, the word deacon is not used in this passage as a noun – to describe their role – but as a verb – to depict their function. The Seven were never called deacons in the modern sense of the word. The task entrusted to them was far more elaborate than that. They were tapped to fix a deficiency in the system that fed thousands of people each day.

The Early Church was having a food distribution problem (Acts 6:1) that caused some widows to be neglected. Because these widows were part of an ethnic group that until recently had been despised, tensions rose to the point of menacing the unity of the brethren. Worse yet, this happened "while the disciples were increasing in number," posing a threat to such growth.

The Twelve indicated that it was not desirable for them to neglect the Word of God in order to serve tables. Because of this reference to serving tables we have assumed that the Seven were to do that. However, the criterion was to find men of good reputation (character), full of the Spirit (spirituality), and of wisdom (capacity for the job at hand) to be put in charge of this task (managers). The moment The Seven were appointed, "the number of the disciples continued to increase greatly in Jerusalem" (Acts 6:7). In other words, the threat to the expansion of church ceased to exist.

Most likely, The Seven were selected because of their proven ability as businessmen, to find a way to fix the flaw in the distribution problem. There is no record that any of them served tables. In fact, two of them exited the picture shortly afterwards: Stephen went to heaven and Phillip left on an extensive evangelistic tour that transformed several cities and sent a Finance Minister as a missionary to his native land. Afterwards, Phillip settled permanently in Caesarea (Acts 11:8).

The main point is that a problem significant enough to be highlighted in the Scriptures was solved with great efficiency because recognized leaders in the congregation were appointed to partner with the Apostles.

Efficiency is the Norm in the Marketplace

Time and again, I have seen that when business people are brought on board as ministry peers, problems that have frustrated pastors for years are solved in a matter of days. Efficiency is the hallmark of marketplace leaders. The competitive environments in which they operate do not allow room for error, or even vacillation, because if too many deals go wrong they will be fired. These folks do not have the "luxury" of telling the board or the shareholders, that "it was the Will of God that we lose the deal;" or, that "the devil interfered with our plans." They need to operate consistently at the highest level of efficiency possible.

When the natural ability to identify the bottom line and to troubleshoot are framed by a personal good reputation, faith, and wisdom, "the Word of the Lord spreads and the number of disciples increase." The impact was so great that even groups, that until then had been unresponsive, got saved, "and a great many of the priests were becoming obedient to the faith" (Acts 6:7). This is due to the influence they had beyond that of the traditional clergy, as far as the city proper was concerned.

Jesus' focus on marketplace movers and shakers, who were not members of the contemporary religious clique, was intentional and deliberate. His objective was to create a new social vehicle – The Church. It was meant to be a movement that freely expanded and not a monument to be gazed at.

Paul's Focus on the Marketplace Shook Cities

From Paul's early missionary trips, we learn that he first went to the synagogue upon arriving in a new city. However, the record of synagogues becoming churches is meager. In most cases, Paul and his band of new believers had to exit under duress. This happened so many times that even Paul gave up on the synagogues and announced that he was going to go to the Gentiles. From this point on we see a succession of power encounters in the marketplace leading to the conversion of masses of new believers.

What happened at Ephesus was not exceptional, but rather normative. In fact, it became a prototype emulated in other cities where the gospel was preached with power in the marketplace. The economy of Ephesus was demon based. Paul and his two partners, Aquila and Priscilla entered the marketplace by setting up a shop while teaching and preaching about the kingdom of God.

Marketplace Jesus

Eventually, a power encounter took place that caused everyone in Ephesus and the surrounding area to hear the Word of God (Acts 19:10). Apparently, it did not stop there because later on Paul and his band were accused of having done the same thing "all over Asia" (Acts 19:26).

The power encounter in Ephesus destroyed the economy of a city that was dependent on witchcraft. Had Paul remained confined to the synagogue, he would have never impacted a region so vast as the one he did by becoming part of the marketplace. What took place in Ephesus was significant because it transformed the city through a power encounter in the marketplace.

CHAPTER 9

The God of Ministry Is Also The God of Business

The vast majority of the Old Testament heroes were not ascetics, but business people deeply involved in everyday issues. Abraham, "the father of the faith," carried that spiritual mantle without giving up his earthly occupation. He was indeed a very prosperous herdsman, so were his sons, his grandsons, and all his great-grandchildren. Job, the head of a family business, was the wealthiest man in the country of Uz (Job 1:3), and was deeply involved in societal and governmental issues (Job 31). Most prophets in the Old Testament, with the notable exceptions of Eli and Samuel, were businessmen, who supported themselves from sources other than the Temple. They saw the hand of God in their business deals, as much as they saw it around the altar. David is a classic example. God provided security services for his shepherding business by empowering him to kill the lions and bears that came to decimate his inventory. To him, God's protection was part of his business.

The Tiny Caterer and the Giant

One of the greatest victories recorded in the Bible pitted this small businessman against a professional soldier. Goliath had immobilized the people of God through sheer intimidation. This went on for forty days until David, a junior partner in a family owned business who had taken a brief stint as a caterer (he went to the battlefield to deliver food), showed up (II Sam. 17:15-19). He arrived in time to hear Goliath's challenge and to see Saul's soldiers flee in total panic. Because he was a godly man, he became incensed by Goliath's taunt to the armies of the living God (I Sam. 17:26). But, because he was a businessman, what caught his attention next was that a reward (profit) had been offered, "What will be done for the man who kills this Philistine?" he asked. He seemed to be saying "There is no way Goliath can ever win because God is on our side. This deal is a sure thing. Why let a good reward go to waste?"

The God of Ministry is a God of Business

David saw no conflict or incompatibility between a spiritual assignment and a financial reward. Unfortunately, years later, when we retell the story we emphasize David's zeal for the Lord, but intentionally suppress any mention of his interest in the recompense, as if the latter was an evil deed. This represents a great injustice, because dichotomizing the spiritual and the material realms did not enter the mind of David, a man according to God's heart. The parallel he drew between God's protection in his business and in the upcoming encounter with Goliath was absolutely natural to him. He expected God to be with him in both undertakings. He did not see fighting Goliath as a spiritual enterprise and protecting his business as a secular one.

The Myth: Businesspeople Are Not Considered Spiritual

Eliab, David's oldest brother, tried to disqualify him from any role on the battlefield, because of his occupation; "With whom have you left those few sheep in the wilderness? (I Sam. 17:28). He accused David of having impure motives and told him to go back to his business. Eliab did not believe David belonged with the pros. In other words, what he said was, "You have no right to comment on our lack of results because your training is in business. Go back and take care of your business, so that you can keep on funding us, but do not tell us what to do!" David turned away from Eliab and kept asking the same question to others. Obviously, his inquiry had to do with the reward because, "the people answered the same thing as before" (I Sam. 17:30).

David must have kept bringing up the certainty that Goliath could and should be defeated because, "when the words that David spoke were heard, they told them to Saul and he sent for him" (I Sam. 17:31). David knew the deal was morally right; it was a sure thing and it was hugely profitable. Consequently, it should be pursued.

Profit Motive is Not Necessarily Evil

David's interest in the reward must not be overlooked since it touches on a very sensitive issue: profit motive. Profit motive is to a businessperson what the drive to win is to an athlete. No athlete, worth his or her salt, will enter a competition to lose. On the contrary, he expects to win. It is such a determination that allows him to overcome extraordinary obstacles. In the same manner, profit motive provides the drive needed for a businessperson to tackle complex challenges in the marketplace. It is a gift from God that, when exercised within proper boundaries, benefits countless millions.

Of course, an athlete who tries to win at any cost becomes destructive. The same is true of businesspeople whose motivation is to profit no matter what. The drive to win and the desire to make a profit are given by God to provide incentive needed to conquer exceptional challenges.

Perceiving profit motive as evil is what prevents many Christians from making it big in business. This is so, because deep down within, they are unsure that they can be successful and godly at the same time. This ambivalence causes them to get lost in a maze of self-doubt. As a result, they struggle with who they are as businesspeople and have trouble accepting as valid the tool provided by God for them to succeed: profit motive. Most of them remain in business, but give up on the possibility of experiencing the joy of the Lord in it or of succeeding significantly, as if the former was impossible and the latter unattainable or worse yet-evil. This is a terrible way to live. Quite often the expectations imposed on Christian businesspeople resemble how women were treated during the Victorian era in regards to sex. They were supposed to do it, but not to enjoy it. To produce results (children), but not to get too excited about the process lest they become sensuous. Likewise, believers in the marketplace are expected to make a profit, but they are not supposed to feel good about it, for fear of becoming materialistic.

There is nothing wrong, intrinsically, with sex or with profit. God created them for a purpose and the fact that they can be abused should not prevent us from appreciating the divine intent behind each one. God attaches pleasure to vital functions such as procreating and eating to ensure that they are exercised. In the business world, profit motive serves that same purpose. It is the incentive that keeps business happening.

In the case of Christian businesspeople, thwarting this motivation is what the devil is after. By labeling them as "profit driven", in a demeaning way, he succeeds by either keeping them away from the marketplace or by handicapping them with self-doubts if they choose to remain in it. This is why it is refreshing, and even healing, to study David's approach.

Business Experience Applied to Spiritual Challenge

When Saul disqualified David because of his lack of professional training, David brought up a principle he had used successfully in business. He told the king how he went after the lions and bears when they attacked his livestock, how he recovered what was stolen and killed the predators. David's example is the equivalent of modern day shoplifting, except instead of criminal gangs, animals carried it out. Killing bears and lions with bare hands was no small feat, but David told Saul that he was able to do it because God was with him. And the same God was going to be with him as he faced Goliath. David exchanged Saul's armor for the tools of his trade, a staff, sling, and stones. Goliath despised and cursed David because of this. David did not let those insults intimidate him. He was comfortable with his equipment because he had seen God empower him every time he used it to protect his business. The situation at hand was no different. The same anointing that operated against the enemies while shepherding should also work against the champion of the enemy. And it did!

God Loves the World and Cares About It

It is necessary to rediscover the principle behind David's approach. He saw God deeply interested in everything he did, whether it was playing the harp, watching his flock, catering food for the soldiers, or fighting the evil giant. His job was his ministry and his ministry was his job.

Nowadays, we have dichotomized the material and the immaterial worlds. We have wrongly concluded that the intangible realm is more likely to be filled with "good" things, while the tangible world, the one where men and women spend the totality of their earthy life, is intrinsically evil. This distinction is not found in the Scriptures.

God created the world and every material thing in it. God loves the world so much that He gave His only begotten Son to provide the means of salvation from the evil, introduced from the outside by the devil. God is compassionate about all of His creation.

Consider the case of Nineveh in Jonah's days. God cared not just about the people, but also the animals in the city (John. 4:11). It is true that the world has been contaminated by sin and that a preponderance of such causes it to deteriorate. But it is also true that "If God's people humble themselves and pray, and seek God's face after turning from their wicked ways, God will hear their prayers, will forgive their sin and God will heal the land!" (II Chron.7: 14). The land this verse talks about is the one we live in. And, not just the land, but also the economy sustained by it, and everything else that sin has defiled. No one appreciates more the need for the healing of the land than those in the marketplace who must live with the consequences brought about by sin.

The Devil Fears Marketplace People

The devil is afraid that business people will discover their God-appointed destiny in the marketplace and bring healing to it. This is why he constantly tries to disqualify them by debasing their occupation, telling them that it is less spiritual than church work. To reinforce this scheme, he paints them as evil and devoid of spirituality. The devil fears the knowledge of the city and the operational efficiency that businesspeople are capable of bringing to Kingdom expansion.

This efficiency is vividly illustrated by the no-nonsense approach of the centurion pleading for Jesus to help his sick servant. He was very appreciative of Jesus' time and did not want to waste any of it. He understood authority systems and how to delegate power. "Lord, just say the word and my servant will be healed. For I, too, am a man under authority, with soldiers under me and I say to this one 'Go', and he goes, and to another 'Come' and he comes." Jesus was so impressed by the centurion's approach that He bestowed on him an extraordinary compliment "I have not found such great faith with anyone in Israel" (Matt. 8:1-10).

Your Divine Destiny is in the Marketplace

Jesus stated that this marketplace leader had a level of faith He had not seen in the religious circles of Israel. Businesspeople take heart! You have the same spiritual capacity that the Roman Centurion had, and even more so, because you live on this side of Calvary and the Resurrection (John 14:12-14). Do not let the devil talk you down. Do not let him confine you to a spectator's seat inside a building wrongly called the church. If you do, he will remain in control of the city.

However, the day you discover that you have a divine call along with the anointing and the jurisdiction to exercise it in the marketplace, God's kingdom will begin to replace Satan's kingdom in the heart of the city. This is what Satan fears indeed.

Be a Businessperson for the Glory of God

This is why it is so important not to let the evil one disqualify you on account of your occupation. He will tell you time and time again that you are a businessperson who has no right to meddle in ministry. Being in business, solely to make money, has no transcendent purpose. But being a businessperson for the glory of God, adds the most sublime purpose to your occupation. Do not let your business limit your destiny, but instead allow your destiny to shape your business by turning it into your ministry.

To do this, a compelling understanding and embracing of God's purpose is crucial, especially if you find yourself in difficult straits. Do not let negative circumstances or difficulties immobilize you. Do not be an echo of disappointing factors when, with God's help, you can be a prophetic voice that calls into being what is still unseen. God's purpose is immutable and you have the full power of heaven at your disposal to fulfill it (John 14: 14).

Fix your eyes on the goal and get going by faith right away. The key is to get going. Jesus began as a carpenter; David as the shepherd of a small flock; Peter as a fisherman; but, they all fulfilled their destinies. Jesus, the carpenter, hung on a tree and carved the lives of millions into replicas of Himself. David became the shepherd of Israel and Peter turned into the premier fisherman of men.

At this point, your question may be: How do I know my place of ministry and if the marketplace is my venue, then how do I function effectively? Listen to the Holy Spirit now. Let Him touch the innermost part of your soul and bring light to those areas darkened by shame and confusion. Never let circumstances define your destiny. Instead, let God remind you of your purpose in life so that you can change the circumstances. Your purpose in life will unfold as you begin to understand the context and capacity in which God has called you to function. Understanding context and capacity gives you liberty to minister effectively in the marketplace.

CHAPTER 10

Context & Capacity

II Timothy 1:9
"Who have saved us, and called us with an holy calling, not according to our works, but according to his own purpose and grace, which was given us in Christ Jesus before the world began..."

This text shows two dimensions of God's involvement in our lives: our salvation and callings. Each one is driven by God's purpose and grace concerning us. It is not because of anything that we have done, but because His purpose and grace were given to us in Christ Jesus before the beginning of time, "before the world began." What we are called to be in the earth is not a consequence of our being born. Our births were necessary so that what God ordained for us could be manifested. His purpose and grace provide the context and the capacity for our individual callings.

What is Context?

According to Webster's Dictionary, it is "The arrangement and union of constituent parts of any structure that characterizes or appropriates purpose. The parts of a written or spoken statement that precede or follow a specific word." For our purposes, context is what follows the word that God announces. Context spells relevance and accuracy and brings appropriate definition. It does not allow you to create something that is not correct as if it is correct. Context causes us to take full advantage of purpose. If we take anything out of context, we do not take advantage of the purpose for which it is given. The whole point of context is to make sure that we do not distort purpose.

What is Capacity?

Let me deal with capacity first as it relates to grace. Grace is charis-something that God does that we have not merited. Grace is God's ability. When we have the grace of God working in our lives, we have God's ability working in us. Only God can satisfy and fulfill Himself.

In this season, we must live our lives in the perfect will of God. To live your life in any other context will lead to God not being pleased. According to Romans 12:2, "...that ye may prove what is that good and acceptable and perfect, will of God."

The Third Dimension

There are three dimensions of God's will. The third dimension is the sovereignty of God. We have to move into the place where our lives are completely God-controlled. When you accept Jesus, your whole life must be lived in a spiritual context. We have made choices because we have been allowed to live our lives according to His good and acceptable, but there is a place where the good and acceptable no longer satisfies. There is a place where you want, what God wants. You do not just want it on Sunday Morning, you want it every day of the week. So you do not spiritualize days and feasts. To give God what He wants you live your life like every day is the day of Sabbath unto the Lord. You do not wait for special days. You have learned to live your life in the context of His will daily

Living Our Lives in the Capacity of Our Purpose

When we start living our lives in the context of our purpose, we will find out that our capacity changes. Our capacity is limited because we have not been living our lives in the right context. Wrong context means limited capacity. If you are not in purpose, God does not have to fuel what you are doing. When I change my context, I make available another dimension of capacity for God to live in my life. He cannot anoint me outside the context of my purpose. **He only is committed to anointing His purpose in your life.** When you come into alignment with His purpose you have the capacity to produce that which is pleasant to God. He takes the limits off and you are only limited by God himself.

Now this means that He has no responsibility to bless anything that He did not ask for. If you ask God to bless it because it is what you longed for, that is idol worship. Whenever the Lord starts to shift you and you agree with God, you will realize that those things that are good, but are not God, need to be sacrificed. This affects every area of our lives. We cannot just limit this to the spiritual realm. Most of us live our lives in the outer court of our being. Our lives have been given to us to manifest different levels of our being. "I be what God says I be and I be it now."

Ask Yourself These Questions:

1. Where am I in manifesting who God says I be? Is it the marketplace?
2. Where am I in my contextual presentation and my capacity?

Most of us are trying to find our total fulfillment in the local church. There are 168 hours in a week. Do we tithe God our time in church? Where are you giving God a first fruits offering? How are you recognizing God? Where are you spending the majority of the time? If we do not properly contextualize the hours that we are not in church, He will never maximize our capacity to be what He says we be in the marketplace.

When you discover and start living your purpose, it is the most fulfilling place you can be and it offers magnificent rewards. Most people do not have a statement of purpose. We know purpose, but we cannot articulate it; and we struggle with the concept. Whenever we think of purpose, we become religious. We must create a statement of purpose and live our lives according to it. It may have nothing to do with ministry, but it has everything to do with why God has given you purpose and grace. Only in that context will He give you the maximum capacity for living.

What Purpose Do You Face In the Morning?

We are called according to a purpose that we face every morning. And we have to admit that few of us are called to full time ministry. God gave man function then form. Form always follows function. We want form, then we want to find function to fit it. "Give me a costume and I will perform. Call me what you will and that is what I will be." But this is not the will of God. If my statement of purpose is to help people, I can serve that purpose as a banker or real estate agent. Do I have to be called to preach to serve that purpose? No, and in the proper context I can make myself available to God to increase my effectiveness.

Be Confident

When I understand purpose, I do not have to look for it in the few hours that I am in church. What if my statement of purpose is to inspire people to live in the highest context of love and joy? I can do that as a funeral director. I do not need to be an elder. This is not about a calling to ministry. This is about how you spend your life 365 days a year. You will please God when you live your life in the context in which He made you and as your context changes there is an equal increase in capacity. God will not set you up for failure. He uses process to mature you, not to fail you.

You can be confident based on your purpose. You do not have to be doing what someone else is doing. We can be confident in the fact that we are fulfilling purpose. You may not be making an enormous amount of money, but you can be happy because you are living out your purpose. Your motivation is from within and you are following an inner voice. It is not robbery to be a blessing to somebody else and it does not have to be in the church. It can be in the marketplace.

I am confident in the fact that I am fulfilling purpose. This is the context in which I live my life most of the time. When I am not in this place, I have allowed people to force me into a context where they want me to be and unfortunately, they will resist any other presentation of me. You have to be committed to operating in the context in which the Lord has ordained for you. Where are you? In what place has He called you to manifest? It is all about discovering and living out your purpose? There are three levels or three states of being in which each of us is currently residing:

THE THREE STATES OF BEING

STATE OF AWAKENING
- Explores "win-win" behavior
- Becomes intuitive
- Takes conscious risks
- Learns to give more instead of taking
- Begins to share feelings
- Thinks through situations, uses reason

STATE OF ALLOWING
- Accepts life unconditionally
- Portrays invisible leadership skills
- Harmless to all
- Has personal power, lives each day with no judgment and accepts truth without blaming others

STATE OF SELF-RELIANCE
- High self-esteem and inner validation
- Motivation from within
- Follows "Inner Voice"
- Is free from all needs and gives selfless service to others
- Experiences no resistance

State of Self-Reliance

State of Allowing

State of Awakening

LEVELS OF BEING

A Closer Look

STATE OF AWAKENING
CHILD STAGE

This level is simply characterized by an encounter with the Lord. Our lives are lived out based on directives given to us by others. We do things for approval. We are attention seekers who are also defensive and fearful. Likewise we are possessive, territorial, controlling, and aggressive.

Our relationships are mechanical, not relational. We have to be motivated and inspired to learn because we do not understand the power of information. At this level there is no desire to improve your life in any arena, primarily because you have no idea that there is more.

There are a surprising number of people who are stuck at this level because they are not aware that there is more in God than what they are receiving. Life is routine for them. Their biggest concern is security and survival and they often blame others for their lack of success. "Just let me hold down a job and watch my finances carefully and I can survive." But this is the child's stage.

Some people will live their lives out at this level of being, and whether we like it or not, we cannot get frustrated with them. We have to accept the fact that everyone will not move out of this stage. They would not know what to do if they moved from the survival mode. I have lost friends because I decided to move from this place. There was a disparity between what I saw was my context and capacity for living and theirs. This level is not wrong; it's choice.

However, it is not a healthy choice.

If you want to move from this place, there has to be vertical movement. Ladders do not move horizontally, they move vertically. Horizontal moves give you more involvement, but it produces the same stuff, just more of it. People who want to survive financially will get another job, but that is not a vertical move, that's horizontal. You are working two jobs, but you cannot denote any change. Nothing changed vertically as it relates to your thinking and principles. You tried to solve the problem without changing.

STATE OF ALLOWING
ADOLESCENT STAGE

People at this level are held back by guilt and self-doubt. We are saved and are willing to broaden our context, but we cannot move into it because we are still dealing with unresolved issues. We are characterized by self-centeredness and low self esteem and are often preoccupied with seeking the approval of others.

We do not believe that God has more for us because we do not believe that we have the capacity for the new context. So we are constantly starting and stopping projects and never accomplishing anything. If you are merely driven by adrenalin, when the adrenalin goes, so will the task.

We have to realize that every time God shifts us, He provides us with the ultimate amount of grace. This should be a level that you pass through quickly it is part of the process.

STATE OF SELF-RELIANCE
ADULT STAGE

This stage is like the inner court; you do not have to slay a lamb. As you encounter the altar and the table of shewbread, you come to

Marketplace Jesus

a level of maturity, but you still have not optimized His presence.

It is a place of confidence in where you are and because of that you are able to take conscious risk. For example, you can share your feelings without fear. At this level, there is a search for meaningful existence; therefore, you do not live your life in "la-la land." Instead, you live your life on purpose. Your life is purpose driven.

At this level, we are fully conscious and awake. We are not oblivious to what is going in us and around us and are sensitive about who comes into our lives. What is on the inside of us is precious; therefore, we realize that we have to guard it. We understand our value and demonstrate total integrity in every thing we do. We are not attached to events to gain feelings of importance or recognition. We are self-reliant and are driven by destiny. We are not just wondering around, we have a destination.

Where are you on the ladder?

Are you in the stage of awakening, allowing or self reliance? Nothing will change until you change. No one can establish purpose for you. God can only speak to you concerning your purpose. Divine purpose drives divine capacity.

Where you are could be part of the process; it could be a means to an end. Do not discount it as not being God. Do not despise the marketplace! It could be where God is calling you to be the Church in the Kingdom.

Discovery and Living Your Purpose

The ten questions below were formulated to help determine whether your life is centered in purpose. Each question will help you clarify a definition of purpose that works for you. Before responding think about each question and read the comments. Check "yes," "don't know/not sure" or "no."

1. Do you recognize what you are good at and what energizes you?
   ____Yes   ____Do not know/ Not Sure   ____No

Many people never find their niche because they avoid analyzing their career objectives. They fall into jobs and never actually ask themselves, "What do I do well? What type of life do I want to lead? What type of work creates positive energy for me?" It's important for you to know and use your skills.

2. Do you fully utilize your most-enjoyed skills?
   ____Yes   ____Do not know/ Not Sure   ____No

Many people stagnate in their jobs. They are capable of doing so much more, yet they are afraid to challenge themselves. There are four separate categories of job expectations. Unfortunately, most people fall into the first three.
   a. It's just a job. Any job is okay as long as the pay is good and I can do my own thing after work."
   b. "Work has to be regular. I need the benefits vacations and security of a permanent job."
   c. " I want substance and content in my profession, trade or vocation. I want to use my talents and be challenged."
   d. "Work is related to money; work is a path to learning and personal growth. Work focuses me on some thing that I really believe needs to be done in this organization, community, or world."

3. Does your work further some interest or issue that you deeply care about?
   ____Yes   ____Do not know/ Not Sure   ____No

Caring is the basis of all-purpose. It requires openness to everything around you. To develop care you need awareness. You should not be burdened by a sense of duty or obligation. When you care naturally, it's because something has profoundly touched and moved you.

4. Do you see yourself, through work, as making a difference in the world?
   ____Yes   ____Do not know/ Not Sure   ____No

The burn-out syndrome is prevalent in today's society. Because so many find work to be meaningless, they lose motivation. Work must offer more than money and status; it must offer you the chance to make a difference.

5. Do you view most days with a sense of enthusiasm?
        ____Yes   ____Do not know/ Not Sure   ____No

When you are serving a purpose larger than yourself, you will feel more committed and become more enthusiastic. Remember, the years fly by quickly, so approach each day
and each task with zeal.

6. Have you developed your own philosophy of life and success?
        ____Yes   ____Do not know/ Not Sure   ____No

Everyone needs a set of principles to live by. Too many people, however, accept the values of others and never develop their own. They do not reflect enough upon their lives, instead, they worry about getting approval from others. Real power comes from acting out your deep personal values.

7. Are you taking the necessary risks to live your philosophy?
        ____Yes   ____Do not know/ Not Sure   ____No

No one is ever completely sure of the path to follow, but those with the courage to believe in themselves and their ideas, with the potential of some loss involved are the true individuals. You must take risk—have the courage to be true to yourself.

8. Do you feel a sense of meaning and purpose for your life?
    ____Yes   ____Do not know/ Not Sure   ____No

You must raise your own expectations of what you can be. You can choose to focus your vigor on what gives you the deepest feeling. You can occupy your time and talents with people, commitments, ideas and challenges that feel purposeful.

9. Do you have active goals this year relating to your purpose?
    ____Yes   ____Do not know/ Not Sure   ____No

Purpose as part of our lives serves as inspiration. But it is really our goals that motivate us on a day to day basis. Our lives are empty when we do not have something to strive for. Goals, though not always easy to achieve, provide the satisfaction of accomplishment which in turn enhances our sense of self-worth.

10. Are you living your life to the fullest now instead of hoping that things will work out someday?
    ____Yes   ____Do not know/ Not Sure   ____No

Why wait for the lottery? Use your potential now instead of taking it to the grave. Now is the time to live within your values, and with purpose.

Score Your Results

For each
"Yes" give yourself a 0
"Not sure or don't know" a 1
"No" a 2

Now add up your score. Since these questions are subjective, there are no right or wrong answers. So use the scoring analysis as a general guideline. Here's how it works.

If you scored between 0-7, your life is pretty focused, you have a sense of direction and you are intent on making a difference.

If you scored between 8-15, you have a sense of purpose, but you need to clarify your commitment. The question is: Are you really living your values and "walking the talk" everyday?

If you scored between 16-20, you run the risk of not using your potential and wasting your life. Please note: This high score may also mean that you are in the middle of a crisis or major transition.

Now that you have had an opportunity to think about what purpose means to you, construct a one sentence statement that captures the essence of your life's purpose as you currently see it.

Choose your words carefully and be specific.

Here are some examples:

"To help as many people as I can during my lifetime, in a way that significantly improves their lives."

"To inspire and empower people to live their highest vision in a context of love and joy."

Marketplace Jesus

My Statement of Purpose

Use this page to write your statement of purpose:

_____

_____

_____

_____

_____

_____

_____

_____

_____

_____

_____

To reinforce your purpose, embrace this statement everyday.

Arise!!

Go Forth With the Anointing God Has Given You For The Marketplace!

A Plan of Assurance for Those in the Marketplace

1. Seek the will of God concerning the purpose for which you were created. It does not have to be anything "deep."

2. Find a career that you love and that will allow you to start living out that purpose.

3. Pursue each day's activities knowing that you are on assignment. You are the church in the kingdom.

4. As you attend your local church, gain the equipping and empowerment you need to return to the work- place as the church in the kingdom.

5. As you mature, both in Christ and in your vocation recognize your sphere of rule and influence in the workplace.

6. Based on your sphere of rule and influence, pursue growth and effectiveness in the ascension gift ministry that flows in your life. Answer the question, "Is my primary role to this job mostly in the area of governing/apostolic; guiding/prophetic; gathering/evangelistic; guarding/pastoral; or growing/teaching?"

7. Never confuse what's Caesar's and what's the Lord's. You don't go to work "to be" the church; you go as the church.

8. If you are in management, make your spiritual covering aware of it. Share with them anything that effects your kingdom assignment, so that he/she can keep you covered.

9. Research and become familiar with those in the Bible and others in the marketplace that have or have had kingdom assignments similar to yours.

10. Just as you daily employ your educational, vocational, and other life experiences to perform your job with excellence, learn likewise to use all the gifts of the Spirit that are available to you, as the church in the kingdom.

11. Stay open to what God may say next! Give Him thanks in Every Thing!

CPSIA information can be obtained at www.ICGtesting.com
Printed in the USA
BVOW071339230112

281074BV00001B/7/A